Cartha

Building Identity
A Handbook
for Architectural
Design

 PARK BOOKS

Building Identity
The Case of Dwelling

Editorial

During his many years in France, the American sculptor George Grey Barnard acquired a large number of Gothic and Romanesque architectural elements from decayed villages in the countryside. Columns, arches, doors, rooms, and whole buildings made up his growing lot. In 1930, during one of Barnard's financial crises, he sold his collection to John D. Rockefeller Jr. The notorious American tycoon, in one of his many philanthropic initiatives, decided to move the collection to the USA and integrate it into the Metropolitan Museum of Art as a sort of subdivision dedicated to Medieval art: the Met Cloisters. From 1934 to 1939, the cloisters of Cuxa, Saint-Guilhem, Bonnefont, and Trie were dismantled and transported to Fort Tryon Park in upper Manhattan. The architect of the new museum, Charles Collens, was given the task of reconstructing the cloisters using only the architectural elements contained within the collection. Through processes of appropriation and rejection of specific parts of the four cloisters, the assimilation of meanings and constructive principles, and the final conciliation of each piece, Collens created a new model for the cloister – an eclectic assemblage representing an entire European typology.

Beyond any criticism regarding the context and ethics of the Met Cloisters, the focus is on the intention it represents to build a new identity by making use of previously existing elements. The project by Charles Collens seems to corroborate the possibility of making a seemingly direct analogy between the sociological theories of Jacques Lacan – among others – regarding the building of one's own identity and the design of an architectural project solely through the interaction with pre-existing traces and conditions. It also raises questions regarding the role of the architect in the project's process:

is Collens the author of the Met Cloisters?

This book, stemming from the Cartha's 2018 cycle, approaches the possibility of a design methodology based on four "identity processes" – Appropriation, Assimilation, Denial, and Conciliation – borrowed from the Lacanian perspective on the makings of one's identity. It takes the form of a handbook, a soft manual for architectural design, clearly structured into two sections: Processes and Projects.

In the first part, each of the four proposed identity-building processes is expanded upon through an interview with an architect or architectural historian whose work hints at a certain affinity to the respective process: Maarten Delbeke and Assimilation, Frederike Lausch and Appropriation, Léon Krier and Rejection, Jonathan Sergison and Conciliation. Their contributions set the foundation for each process to be utilized as a productive tool in a hands-on *Entwurf* (engl. draft).

As for the Projects section, the practices Made in, Sam Jacob Studio, Monadnock, Bruther, Bureau Spectacular, Studio Muoto, and Conen Sigl were invited to take on a task similar to the one Collens undertook. The aforementioned identity-building processes acted as guidelines for the design process, challenging the architects to each design a new dwelling (house, apartment, manor, hut, etc.), drawing on projects inserted into their own conceptual, social, and physical contexts but not designed by them.

The results of this speculative design exercise, beyond featuring a richness of references and depth of understanding of the meaning of previously built projects, promote a reflection on the contexts and situations the invited architects face. Interests in the current notions of social interaction, ideas of property, drastic shifts in environmental conditions, and conceptions of history and future are brought forth in critical, seductive ways. The virtuosity displayed in the projects thus allows us to answer the question of authorship, for the creation of new meanings is indeed the emergence of a new identity, therefore of an independent person, a self.

It is not our intention to present an approach to architecture through identity as a definitive path, rather to propose it as an enriching complementary analysis and project methodology. The notion of identity, as proposed by Cartha's 2018 cycle and by this book, forces one to adopt a critical position towards a context. It promotes a deep understanding of what the "now" is by asking why it is so, what has been rejected if this has been appropriated, what has been lost in the constant processes of assimilation, and what the outcome of a more conciliatory approach might be.

Processes

Assimilation
 Maarten Delbeke
Appropriation
 Frederike Lausch
Rejection
 Léon Krier
Conciliation
 Jonathan Sergison

Assimilation   Editorial   9

Assimilation: The absorption and integration of people, ideas, or culture into a wider society or culture. The process of becoming similar to something. The process of taking in and fully understanding information or ideas.[1]

Since its foundation in 1865 by British banker Thomas Sutherland, the Hongkong and Shanghai Banking Corporation (HSBC) has changed its headquarters four times. Curiously, all four headquarters were built on the same plot at Victoria Bay in Hong Kong; each version was demolished and replaced with a new building and new branding strategy to reflect Hong Kong's shifting identity from colonial economy to a significant participant in the global free market.

    The first version, a neoclassical building in the fashion of its European contemporaries, opened the road to a full assimilation of Western architecture in the area, becoming one of the main examples of the neoclassical style in the Far East. Twenty years later, the building was demolished and replaced by a larger project in the Victorian style, following the trend of colonial architecture in the British Empire. This headquarters would last until 1934, when Hong Kong became an important player in the proto-globalized economy, consequently requiring a larger and more modern building. More than ten storys high, the new Art Deco headquarters stylistically mirrored its North American counterparts. Finally, rushing to be assimilated by growing global capitalism during the 1970s, Hong Kong developed into a major international financial center. Once again, the building proved insufficient, and in 1978 was torn down and replaced with their current headquarters by Foster + Partners in 1986. The project became one of the most explicit examples of a developing region's eagerness to be assimilated into an external idea of a global market, adopting the skyscraper as a symbol of the emerging economy in Asia.

The HSBC headquarters enacts two conditions of assimilation in architecture: as the physical presence of a foreign reigning power – in the case of the first neoclassical and Victorian versions – or as a voluntary desire to be perceived as part of a global identity, culminating in the current techno-corporate tower by Foster + Partners. Assimilation is a double-edged process, actively used by both the ones who wish to assimilate and by those who wish to be assimilated.

Although Assimilation, like the processes of Appropriation, Rejection, and Conciliation, has been a constant throughout history, its specific duplicity highlights its relevance in the current moment, as the number of forces, of wills, which influence our perspectives and decision-making seem to be at an all-time high.

1 Based on the definition provided by the Oxford Dictionary

1. In your opinion, what are the defining traces of contemporary society's identity, in either a global or local context?

> In the Western context, the only one I can claim any familiarity with: a tendency towards self-absorption, with the attendant prevalence of identity politics and primary emotional reac- tions, such as indignation or outrage, over rationality. I find it striking how genuine and crucial emancipatory movements – regarding such issues as all aspects of identity – have transformed into issues that are so easily manipulated by both consumerism and populism, all while humanity as a whole is facing literally existential threats.

2. How do you position yourself in regard to these traces?

> I'm conflicted, as I recognize the potential value and variety – as well as necessity – of the trends outlined above, and the potential of new technologies and media to radically change the ways in which we think, interact, and do research. So I try to engage with these questions critically and to the best of my limited ability.

3. Is architecture relevant to the identity building of a society? In which way? Or why not?

> Historically, architecture has legitimized its existence by proclaiming its capacity to express the identity of a society. The fact that buildings are rooted in the soil, often built at least partly from locally available materials, and accommodate customs that can be alleged to be local or particular to a given society has been used since Vitruvius to argue for the necessity of architecture and the need for architecture to reflect the values of society. The fact that this argument has been so pervasive has probably to do with the fact that buildings are

essential to our sense of place, and that many monuments express some notion of political or social order. However, neither "function" is a prerogative of architecture – our sense of place, for instance, is as much informed by "architecture" as by "non-architectural" buildings, by landscapes, smells and sounds, languages and accents, as well as social interactions and events. So I believe that this slippage, turning a very generic sense of how buildings define a particular place in a specific society – or in the life of a random group of individuals – into a prerogative and legitimation of architecture, should be viewed very critically. I do think that the work of the last decade or so of architects and planners thinking about and working with design and planning processes, regulations, real estate development, user participation and such is very relevant, and reflects and possibly transforms processes in society, also because they engage with collectives as opposed to either individuals or abstract entities such as "the city" (as in city branding through architecture), "the region," or "the country."

4. Are you conscious of your role, as an architectural historian, in the building of an architectural and social identity?

As a teacher of architectural history, I have increasingly become aware of that role. On the one hand, because so much of our historical patrimony has come into being through processes involving the construction of political or social identity – which raises the question of exactly how and why architecture enables such construction, and to what extent it makes architecture complicit in sustaining particular power structures. On the other hand, as an architectural historian we tell stories and need to consider not only the subject and plot of our stories, but also who our audience is. It is more diverse, with more varied cultural and intellectual backgrounds than when I studied architecture, and it also has different political sensibilities, some more sophisticated than mine were at their age, but also some less – the latter is especially true with regard to a sense of history, which in my experience has changed radically over the last twenty years. So we need to think about how to make these stories accessible, enticing, and relatable. In my view, this situation does not necessarily entail changing the curriculum per se – I do believe that we have to teach and research things we know something about, through our studies and lived experience, which in my case is the highly canonical European architectural history of around the last 500 years. But it does challenge us to find new kinds of stories as well as new ways of doing history, so our stories can become part of other stories as well.

5. We would like to focus now on a specific identity building process: Assimilation. It is the first process out of the four, we are addressing in this cycle. It entails two different motions: one performed by the ones who wish to be assimilated, and another by the reigning identity which assimilates. How do you see this process and these two moments in the history of architecture, specifically in print?

I find assimilation a very problematic notion, as it implies – as does your question – a duality between a "reigning" identity and another that wishes or has to "assimilate." Our preoccupation with assimilation is perhaps a side effect of an astounding process that has occured in the 1980s and 1990s: a process in which the sophisticated deconstruction of ontologies such as identity resulted in the reification of different identities without any consideration as to what might actually be shared, versus what might be complex and ambiguous if not explicitly flagged as such. At the same time, it should be granted that architecture opens itself up to this question precisely because architecture exists as a cultural practice by its claim to embody the values of a society. In that sense, architecture is almost by definition an attribute of a "reigning" society – see the dedication of Vitruvius to Augustus. Piranesi suggested that the Roman empire fell because the more primitive people coveted its sophisticated architecture; no assimilation here, but conquest. But these are ultimately highly limited perspectives on very complicated historical processes, where roles often reverse and become entangled. Again, it is our task here not to settle on one version of the story, but to keep doubting and asking questions.

This complexity is, I think, well illustrated by the role of print in the diffusion of architectural models. What does it mean when we encounter a Serlian portico in Peru, executed in painted wood? Which of these two motions does it form a part of? The way we answer these questions tells us a lot about our implicit assumptions (for instance, about how we interpret and value sophistication) and the degree to which we want to believe that architecture is capable of exerting hegemony or authority.

Maarten Delbeke holds the Chair of the History and Theory of Architecture at the Department of Architecture at ETH Zurich. He researches and teaches the history and theory of early modern art and architecture in Europe. His research interests include baroque and rococo art and architecture, print culture, origin myths in architecture, and the reception history of early modern art and architecture.
He is active as an architecture critic and is the author of *The Art of Religion. Sforza Pallavicino and Art Theory in Bernini's Rome* (2012/2016), among others, as well as the editor, most recently, of *Sforza Pallavicino. A Jesuit Life in Baroque Rome* (2022).
He is the founding editor-in-chief of *Architectural Histories*, the online journal of the European Architectural History Network (EAHN).

Assimilation　　　　　　　　　　　Interview with Marteen Delbeke　　15

Pierre Paul Sevin (attributed), The Royal Reception of Ambassadors from the King of Siam by His Majesty at Versailles on 1 September 1686, 1687 etching and engraving, 82 × 52 cm

Appropriation: The action of appropriating something. The deliberate reworking of images and styles from earlier, well-known works of art. Taking (something) for one's own use, typically without the owner's permission.[1]

In 1980, the American architect Steven Izenour started designing a vacation home for his father. For this small house, Izenour takes a seemingly common Connecticut cottage and mixes it with elements from classical architecture in a playful interpretation of what he thought his father's house should be. The specificity of this act lies in the freedom Izenour allows himself in the process. For instance, he deprives columns of their materiality and structural function, yet keeps their form – in the case of the porch columns, only their outline – in order to distill these elements to an almost comedic state where they are but an ironic nod to the "real." Throughout the project, the same exercise is repeated, appropriating elements and giving them new functions, proportions, and scales while keeping traces of what defines them. Izenour proposes an original building which feels uncannily familiar but is in fact an empty vessel, waiting to be filled anew. We thus define Appropriation as this condition of simultaneity produced through the co-option and re-articulation of architecture for unanticipated agendas, alternative expectations, and unintended identities.

Within the scope of architecture, Appropriation takes on multiple shapes: the blunt repurposing of structures; the knowledgeable, subtle borrowing of elements; the ill-informed replication of structures or typologies; or simply straightforward copy-pasting of whole buildings into a different context.

[1] Based on the definition provided by the Oxford Dictionary

1. In your opinion what are the defining traces of contemporary society's identity, in either a global or local context?

> First of all, I do not believe in the concept of a stable identity, neither in relation to a society nor in relation to the individual. The concept has proven to be quite dangerous. In the past, and even today when we think of movements like Les Identitaires in France and the German Identitäre Bewegung, the claims made in the name of a particular identity were and are often exclusive and discriminatory. If we think of a society's identity not as something essential but as always forming anew according to the configuration of assemblages, I would rather speak of the discourses and controversies prevailing in a society and of the issues that haunt these debates. Spontaneously, two traces come to mind: on a global scale, I see climate change being a decisive factor in our lives and our conversations; on a local, more personal scale, the complex and difficult German history haunts a lot of the debates, even the ones in architecture. Nationality is not a relevant category for me, but I cannot deny the fact that National Socialism and the GDR register in my thinking as factors to be remembered.

2. How do you position yourself in regard to these traces?

> I am trying and still learning to perceive and write from an embodied and situated perspective. I have a quote by Donna Haraway hanging opposite my desk: "The alternative to relativism is partial, locatable, critical knowledges sustaining the possibility of webs of connections called solidarity in politics and shared conversations in epistemology."[1] Being based in the German discourse, I consider the political involvement of architects to be a fruitful study as it shows that architecture doesn't happen in a political vacuum under purely aesthetic,

constructive, or functional aspects. Politics should never be the exclusive viewpoint, but one to be added to the focus on form, construction, and function. What interests me are the contradictory and changing positions of people trying to live their lives and work, so it's not about assigning a category like "He was a Nazi" to a person, but interpreting the sources that remain from a person's life and seeing how politics constantly entered and changed that life. I should add that I am always committed to anti-fascism and anti-discrimination.

3. Is architecture relevant to the identity building of a society? In which way? Or why not?

Architecture plays a discussed and disputed role in society. How should one deal with buildings from the era of National Socialism? What does the demolition of the Palast der Republik, the former site of the GDR legislature, stand for? Should we rebuild the Berliner Schloss? Do city centers need the reconstruction of old timber-framed houses? These are political debates that have been triggered by architecture, or vice versa, this is where the political becomes apparent in architectural discourses. If we understand identity as a struggle about what is valued in a society and what is not, then architecture, its design (What is to be expressed through this architecture? Who commissions it and why?), its production (Where do the materials come from? Who executes the design?), and its reception (To what discussions and behaviors does this architecture incite?) are relevant factors.

4. Are you conscious of your role as an architect and academic in the construction of an architectural and social identity?

Well, as a lecturer and postdoctoral researcher I participate in discussions about the role of architecture in society and the influence of politics on architecture, but I do not overestimate my influence. My goal is not to construct an architectural and social identity. Rather, I hope that students in my seminars will learn that this concept called "identity" is a contested field and that architects will participate in these debates whether they want to or not. I would therefore suggest not to work on constructing an identity, but to work on making changing multiplicities in architecture and society possible.

5. We would like to focus now on one of the four identity building processes from this cycle of CARTHA: Appropriation. In your research, you have tackled the specifics of a political ideology, and consequent social movement, with a precise take on the form, function, and meaning of architecture. How would you position the notion of Appropriation within the narratives emerging from the relation between fascism and a certain architectural identity?

I have written about how the National Socialist past has been debated in architectural discourse since the 1970s by examining one figure in particular, Max Bächer, his attempt to write a book on fascism and architecture, and his failure to accomplish this. Especially the new rationalist designs by architects such as Aldo Rossi incited harsh debates: is the use of columns an appropriation of the supposed neoclassical Nazi architecture? Central to this new rational architecture was the claim that architecture possessed autonomous principles or forms and this autonomy of forms was understood, especially by Rossi, as an act of resistance against the instrumentalization of architecture by politics. According to this view, elementary forms should be able to be used free of political meaning, that is, colonnades are not automatically an expression of totalitarianism or fascism – an accusation that was often voiced, especially in West Germany of the 1970s. Phoebus Panigyrakis and I wrote a paper on Rossi's design for the German Historical Museum, which was planned but abandoned because of the reunification and whose design sparked a lively debate about what architecture is appropriate to represent Germany's history. Rossi's colonnades were interpreted as an appropriation of the facade of the Haus der Deutschen Kunst, one of the first representative buildings of the Nazi regime, and it was criticized that this way the National Socialist past becomes a sort of normalized set piece in a design that consists of various fragments and abstracted historical appropriations. Thus, because certain architectural forms were read as an expression of National Socialism, the appropriation of these forms was automatically read as a reference to National Socialism, regardless of whether this was intended or not. This reference then became the central point of criticism. Over time, new meanings of forms inscribe themselves, so that it seems absurd to us today that the Neue Staatsgalerie in Stuttgart by James Stirling was also accused of appropriating fascist architecture because it has natural stone facades and columns, although these elements are used playfully – a playfulness that Nazi representational buildings lacked, of course. At that time, however, any form of appropriation was viewed with skepticism.

1 Haraway Donna. "Situated Knowledges: The Science Question in Feminism and the Privilege of Partial Perspective," *Feminist Studies* 14, no. 3 (fall 1988), 575-599; here 584

Frederike Lausch is an architectural historian, post-doctoral research associate at the Technical University Darmstadt and co-founder of the Center for Critical Studies in Architecture. Her research focuses on political implications of architectural discourses and architectural theories in the twentieth century; in particular the reception of radical French theory in architecture (PhD dissertation 2019, transcript 2021) and the German postwar discourse on architecture under National Socialism (mbooks 2021; HPA 7/2021). She currently researches the Communication Centre of Scientific Knowledge for Self-Reliance (CCSK).

Appropriation Interview with Frederike Lausch 23

Frederike Lausch, slides from the archive of the German
Architecture Museum, 2019

Rejection: The dismissing or refusing of a proposal, idea, etc.[1]

The notion of the "new" implicitly relates to a notion of the "old." At the core of how these two concepts respond to each other lies the following: one is different from the other. Though the new does not necessarily replace the old,[2] the notion of improvement it carries might lead to the rejection of the old. When the British forces took the port of Basrah in southern Iraq – eventually making their way up to Baghdad – at the beginning of the twentieth century, they brought with them an approach to citymaking that was dramatically new to the Iraqi context. From 1918 on, the British-controlled Public Works Department (PWD), headed by Major J. M. Wilson, began to draft ambitious plans to "improve" the city of Baghdad, envisioning an adjacent "New Baghdad" that completely disregarded the pre-existing city and its cultural context, drawing only tokenizing connections to a clearly foreign idealization of an ancient Mesopotamian culture. In an effort to make Baghdad an attractive destination for both native British and Indian British, the PWD planned a new city over the preexisting one, using an iron-grid urban morphology and other British urban strategies which had proved successful in previous colonies. A similar approach was used in Basrah where the planners went so far in the new plan, as to name some streets and squares using familiar names such as Piccadilly Circus, Oxford Street, or Jaipur Road. This blatant disregard for the Iraqi context was an uninformed rejection of the existing built environment, as well as of the cultural and social contexts. Aimed at reshaping Iraq in the image of the British empire, it ended up fueling the friction between the different factions of Iraq instead, a friction still to be resolved today. The approach taken by the British during their mandate in Iraq was a tactic of control: using erasure as a form of Rejection to colonize an architectural identity and unravel a built environment. But it is not the only possible approach to Rejection. In the interview with Léon Krier he shares with us his views on the role Rejection plays in his specific approach to the modern movement and to architecture in general, placing this notion as a source of agency and power, which is potentially destructive but also redemptive.

1 Based on the definition provided by the Oxford Dictionary
2 See "Conciliation," p. 37

1. In your opinion What are the defining traces of contemporary society's identity? Either in a global or local context.

> Dependence on fossil and nuclear fuels. Most building materials, building forms and processes, and all urban and architectural designs are defined and dominated by them and so are their life span and their regular destruction through use, redevelopment, and war action. Traditional architecture, be it vernacular building or classical architecture, is characterized by the use of local building materials. Only very seldomly and for extremely important buildings were building materials carted from distant quarries or forests. It is local building materials which shape the different architectural identities of the Basque country or those of Tuscany or Bali. Synthetic building materials, on the other hand, are products of analogous standardized industrial, fossil fuel-dependent processes around the world. The products and their tectonic performances are the same around the globe, largely unifying architectural character and eliminating local identities defined by factors such as soil, climate, and altitude.
>
> It is tragic that more and more intelligent minds should at once be spellbound by that undecipherable, and easily manipulated, spirit of the age (zeitgeist) and so indifferent to the spirit of place (genius loci), the conditions of nature, of gravity, of local climate, topography, soil, customs, all of them phenomena objectively apprehensible in their physical and chemical qualities.

2. How do you position yourself in regard to these traces?

> Like it is the case for most human beings and societies, most of my private and public activities are defined by these energy sources. The practicing of traditional architectures and

urbanism is rendered very difficult and sometimes impossible because building and town planning legislations, building culture generally, are part and parcel of an industrial ideology and mindset. Modernism and suburbanism rule supreme in state and government offices and academia.

My work demonstrates in theory and in practice how traditional architecture and urbanism are practiced and justified in a hostile institutional, academic, and professional climate.

3. Is architecture relevant to the identity building of a society? In which way? Or why not?

Traditional architectures and urbanisms as shaped by soil, gravity, altitude, and climate are instrumental in shaping the identity of societies worldwide. Traditional architectures around the world have over centuries evolved a great variety of building languages. Unlike spoken languages, the elements constituting the traditional building vocabulary need no translation in order to be understood across borders and ages. They have universal validity, are part of technology before and beyond (transcending) mere historical deployments and meanings. Modern traditional builders or designers are naturally polyglots, can within no time decipher and master local idioms and realize structures in harmony with local traditions, culture, climate, soil, altitude. This cultural and technical versatility singularly contrasts with the dumb and blind modernist monoglottism, or rather illiteracy, that imposes the same building types and mannerism across the planet, irrespective of culture, climate, or geography. To build traditionally today is not ignoring the demands of modern life; on the contrary, it is confronting the urgency to adapt to our planet's means. It also answers one of the deepest aspirations of humankind, even more relevant in these transient times, "to belong," by building and preserving a world of beautiful landscapes and splendid towns which imprint on our hearts forever, places we can be proud to come from, to inherit and to pass on to future generations. To practice it, often against overwhelming peer prejudice, bureaucratic chicane, and reigning fashionable fads, demands a challenging intellectual and professional determination.

The generalized use of fossil energies, the mechanization of human productions and relations, and the use of synthetic building materials and air conditioning have temporarily led to ignoring the fundamental conditions of nature. The dominant modernist building typology and suburbanism (the skyscraper, the landscraper, the suburban home and their massive proliferation in geographically segregated monofunctional zones) can only be sustained and serviced in conditions of cheap fossil energies. Very little of the legacy of that collective malpractice will survive the inevitable global consequences of oil scarcity and eventual depletion. The increasing human cost of oil wars announces the end of the fossil fuel age and therefore that of the reign of modernism and suburbanism.

But I would say that, given the present evolutionary stage of the human species, even if there were no limitations for any foreseeable future nor any political problems for the provision of fossil fuels, we should still go back to traditional forms of settlement, agriculture, industry, production, crafts – to those forms which were and remain the ones fitted to the human scale, to our measurements and gregarious nature. Now that too many of our built environs have lost it, we discover that the human scale is an irrenouncable attribute of civilization, not an obsolete luxury. No amount of connectivity, social media, and virtual reality can be a permanent substitute for physical contact in social interactions and its corollary of successful mixed-use open public spaces.

4. Are you conscious of your role, as an architectural historian, in the building of an architectural and social identity?

I am interested in architectural and urban forms of the pre-fossil fuel ages not as irretrievable history but as a technologically, socially, and artistically irrenounceable experience, as resources for the future. I am not an architectural historian, and I have little use for that profession and discipline. I am, to be explicit, not practicing historical designs but traditional architectural and urban designs for modern societies around the globe.

The traditional Persian-Greek-Roman-Christian city is the universal city model for open, modern, and democratic societies. It is the polycentric city of independent communities. In that sense, the architect has the choice to participate in building or in destroying modern democratic society.

The mission of planners and architects should be to look after the local culture and patrimony and work within the local parameters to preserve, rebuild, and enhance their idiosyncrasy with new construction respectful of its context. There are plenty of new traditional urban and architectural projects under construction around Europe and the Americas. They, like the Prince of Wales' Poundbury project, are entirely undertaken by private and individual initiative. Val d'Europe, Plessis-Robinson, Brandevoort, Lomas de Marbella Club, Pont Royal en Provence, Knokke-Heulebrug, Seaside, Windsor and Alys Beach in Florida, Paseo Cayalá in Guatemala. In contrast, contemporary modernist developments, however large or "advanced," like the Apple, Facebook, Google, Masdar megacompounds, are without exception of a suburban nature, horizontal or vertical monothematic sprawl – in general, regarding the latest talk about "smart cities," incorporating the ever-evolving newest technologies of connectivity, what is just a matter of infrastructure should not be confused with urban fabric form and town planning.

We are the first generation to have reacted to the cataclysmic modernist devastation of the world by building an operative critique backed by a general theory for a human-scale architecture and urbanism. This model of new traditional architecture and urbanism is being applied worldwide. I had the lucky misfortune to grow up in cities which had been spared war destructions, yet already suffered the tragic consequences of modernist redevelopment policies. As I grew up, I witnessed how the traditional European city was being deconstructed as a social, physical, economic structure, as an ethical and aesthetic space. It is that model which is common to all European nations. It has allowed the open, mixed, modern society to emerge and flourish. It is that city model, inherited from Athens and Rome, which modern societies worldwide desire, but are everywhere admonished by modernist propaganda that they can no longer have, except for vacation and entertainment.

5. We would like to focus now on a specific Identity Building process: Rejection. It is based on the notion of non-identification with the characteristics – formal, conceptual, emotional – of something, leading to its Rejection. Throughout your career, you have taken a clear stance regarding your own notion of how to make architecture. How do you relate to the process of Rejection in your take on other approaches towards architecture? For instance, modernism, futurism or high-tech architecture? Do you completely reject them or do you see relevance in some of their characteristics, within their context?

Modern traditional architecture and urbanism are not motivated by a feeling of rejection but by the urgency of reconstruction. Reconstruction, because modernism has deconstructed architecture and urbanism physically and mentally. I am about to publish the ninth volume of Le Corbusier's complete works called *Le Corbusier after Le Corbusier – LC Translated, Corrected, Completed*, proving that if there is a quality in his work, that quality can be achieved by traditional architectural means, techniques, materials, construction processes. The interesting forms of architectural modernism, futurism, high-tech were without exception pioneered by industrial production, storage, and transportation building design, by driving and flying vehicles design, by machine, weapons, and tool design. They are characterized by an aesthetic which is not place-bound, but purpose- and function-bound. The forms of oil rigs, the monumentality of grain stores, the beauty of cooling towers, and the aerodynamic elegance of an aeroplane don't deliver the typological or formal repertoire for the making of human-scale places, buildings, or cities.

What is commonly called high-tech is uniquely related to fossil-fuel energies and their synthetic materials. I am suggesting that architects and planners become primordially concerned not with the "historicity" of traditional architecture and urbanism, but with their technology, with the techniques of building settlements in a specific geographic location and condition, and hence with local architectural and urban cultures.

The other common belief is that progress, human progress, is necessarily linked to high-technological progress. Technology is the logos of technique. Technology is neither "high" nor "low." What looks "high" superficially may be "low" in ecological terms. I advocate to respect, study, and use traditional ideas where and when they are relevant for the living and essential for our well-being. They are repositories not merely of humanity, but of humaneness and ecology.

New urbanism and modern traditional architecture are to this day the only coherent theories of environmental design based on extremely long-term sustainability, founded on millennial experience. The many architects who practice it do so despite their architectural education and generally against overwhelming academic prejudice, but sustained by wide public support and market demand.

> Léon Krier is a unique voice in today's architectural discourse due to his commitment to developing a relevant and pragmatic theory of architecture based on his own experience and observations of architectural practice and opposed to the easy, abstract theorizing so common in contemporary architectural writing.

Léon Krier, Atlantis Panorama

Conciliation: The action of mediating between two disputing people or groups.[1]

Engineer Giacomo Mattè-Trucco's Fiat Lingotto Factory, opened in Turin, Italy in 1923, was a radical new development in the factory typology. Referencing Albert Kahn's Ford factories in the United States, the reinforced concrete, five-story, 500-meter-long linear assembly line was organized to embody the processes of production. Manufacturing began at the ground level, where nearby rails delivered raw materials; assembly continued in a vertical spiral up through the building until the finished car was delivered onto the roof's race track for a test drive. The completed product would exit the building on one of two monumental ramps, ready for display and sale. The building operated as a factory until the early 1980s, until Fiat S.p.A. held a competition to transform the interior of the factory into an entertainment hub. In 1985, Fiat commissioned the Renzo Piano Building Workshop (RPBW) to convert the factory, adding commercial space, offices, an art gallery, an auditorium, a conference center, and multiple hotels.

Although the exterior remained largely intact to maintain the previous identity of the building, the factory interior was transformed from a space of production into a space of consumption, permitting the coexistence of each iconic program to construct a new architectural identity. A clear understanding of both functions – the overlapping of the demands and intentions of a space of production from the first quarter of the century and the current understanding of spaces of leisure – come together in a new specific formalization. This radical shift of program from one of work into one of leisure has created a situation in which the spaces of the converted factory reflect these design processes of conversion and Conciliation. Despite this otherwise almost seamless conversion, RPBW's most prominent addition to the project, "The Bubble," a spherical glass conference space floating above the factory's roof, is emblematic of the difficulties inherent to the project, an incongruous object of compromise that highlights the complications of mediation and the struggles of resolution.

We posit Conciliation within architecture as a project of negotiation between two parties, a spatial diplomacy that instrumentalizes the apparent incompatibility of two ideologies to produce a new identity.

1 Based on the definition provided by the Oxford Dictionary

1. In your opinion, what are the defining traces of contemporary society's identity, in either a global or local context?

I was born in Great Britain and have lived in London for most of my life. More recently, I have been living in Zurich. My view of the defining traits of contemporary society is therefore inevitably affected by my personal experiences and circumstances. In this sense I feel that European culture is founded on classical principles. Of course, these have also been widely exported through colonialism and Western cultural hegemony. But I am also fascinated by the traces of other cultures that endure as forms of resistance to the dominant cultural paradigm.

2. How do you position yourself in regard to these traces?

As an architect all that I do stems from an implied relationship to the canon of classicism. Nearly all the work we are involved in is located in Europe and we consciously engage with the numerous and often complex local traditions and cultural influences. If we take London as an example, we are dealing with a rich and culturally complex urban context, which has evolved historically as people of different backgrounds settled there. This has been the case throughout the long history of the city, but more so today: London is a truly global city with a very diverse population. The traces this leaves on the urban fabric are there to be read, and we find ourselves drawing upon them rather than denying their existence.

3. Is architecture relevant to the identity building of a society? In which way? Or why not?

Architecture is always creating an image of and for society. The buildings and spaces of a city are central in the creation of the identity of society. The capacity of architecture to offer images that support the ambition of totalitarian regimes is well documented. More recently the commissioning of buildings from well-known architects is seen by some as creating added value.

The city I currently live in, Zurich, bears no trace of such expressions of power and control, and offers an urban expression based on principles of tolerance and collaboration. This is partly why I find it so agreeable.

4. Are you conscious of your role as an architect and professor in the construction of an architectural and social identity?

In my role as an architect I believe that the sum of all we have built in twenty-two years of practice represents a minute addition to the various European cities our projects have added to. However, because our projects have been widely published, I would acknowledge that our work has had a wider influence, although our position in architecture is a marginal one. I am happy with this. I do not believe that I could ever claim to build what would amount to the identity of a society.

The role I have had as a teacher has a much bigger influence, and involves a different form of responsibility. Over the last twenty-five years I have contributed to the education of many hundreds of students, who are now working as architects. While their interests and approaches may differ from my own, I hope that I have helped them find their direction.

5. We would like to focus now on one of the four identity building processes from this cycle of CARTHA: Conciliation. Throughout your practice, the relation between a building and its site is a constant concern through the use of critical interpretation. Might this be a way, in the context of contemporary European urban centers, to conciliate a meaningful architecture with the often contradictory values defined by economical and political interests?

The theme of "reconciliation" is one that we often find ourselves addressing in our work, particularly in relation to the contemporary European city. A clear example of this approach can be found in the apartment building and crèche we realized in Geneva in 2011. In this project we consciously arranged the form and elements of the facades in a manner that interprets the character of the older neighboring buildings that abut it – a nineteenth-century school building and a retail and office building from the 1960s. The two buildings had an ambivalent relationship, which we aimed to reconcile, bridging the gap between them and incorporating them within a bigger urban ensemble. The Basel-based architect Roger Diener once said that "a place can be brought to order through the building of a single house." I believe in this as an ambition.

> Jonathan Sergison is a founding partner of Sergison Bates Architects. Since the beginning of his career in the mid 1990s, he has advocated for an architecture that prioritizes awareness of the place it stands in over spectacularity and uniqueness, mediating the pre-existing conditions of a determined site while still being critical towards it. After twenty-two years of professional practice and twenty-five of teaching, his voice has become highly relevant when talking about Conciliation in the context of architecture.

Conciliation   Interview with Jonathan Sergison   42

Jonathan Sergison, Rue du Cendrier housing and
crèche, Geneva 2011, photograph by David Grandorge

Projects

Made in
Sam Jacob Studio
Monadnock
Bruther
Bureau Spectacular
Studio Muoto
Conen Sigl

L'uomo Vitruviano 2.0

Lucasfilm, *The Empire Strikes Back,* Luke's robot hand, film still

Made in 47

Since its foundation in 2003, Made in has been active in competitions, construction and research projects. Based in Geneva, Made in works on both a national and international level, developing proposals in urban contexts, complex infrastructures, and demanding programs of all scales and natures.

The embedding in a humanistic environment and the critical questioning of today's construction tasks are of central importance. The sociocultural relevance of the architect's tasks in the urban context is always precisely analyzed in light of its permanently changing nature. The interaction between a site, a specific client, and a dynamic environment opens possibilities of innovative pro- grammatic solutions that have come to constitute the core of Made in's proposals.

Beyond their ongoing engagement as founding partners of the architectural practice, Patrick Heiz and François Charbonnet devote themselves intensively to academical research and teaching. After numerous guest professorships in Switzerland and abroad, they have been teaching as full professors at ETH Zürich since 2018 as full professors.

L'uomo Vitruviano 2.0 — Made in — 48

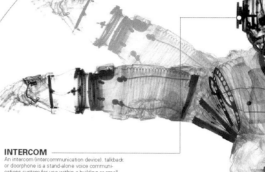

BOW WINDOW
A bow window or compass window is a curved bay window. Bow windows are designed to create space by projecting beyond the exterior wall of a building, and to provide a wider view of the garden or street outside and typically combine four or more casement windows, which join together to form an arch, differentiating itself from the more common bay window which typically features 3 casement windows.

INTERCOM
An intercom (intercommunication device), talkback or doorphone is a stand-alone voice communications system for use within a building or small collection of buildings, functioning independently of the public telephone network (Azori 2016).

COOLING TOWER
A cooling tower is a heat rejection device that rejects waste heat to the atmosphere through the cooling of a water stream to a lower temperature. Cooling towers may either use the evaporation of water to remove process heat and cool the working fluid to near the wet-bulb air temperature or, in the case of closed circuit dry cooling towers, rely solely on air to cool the working fluid to near the dry-bulb air temperature.

SAFETY LOCK
A lock is a mechanical or electronic fastening device that is released by a physical object (such as a key, keycard, fingerprint, RFID card, security token, coin etc.), by supplying secret information (such as a number permutation or password), or by a combination thereof.

WATER CLOSET
A flush toilet is a toilet that disposes of human excreta (urine and feces) by using water to flush it through a drainpipe to another location for disposal, thus maintaining a separation between humans and their excreta.

INSULATION
Thermal insulation is the reduction of heat transfer (i.e. the transfer of thermal energy between objects of differing temperature) between objects in thermal contact or in range of radiative influence. Thermal insulation can be achieved with specially engineered methods or processes, as well as with suitable object shapes aid materials.

L'uomo Vitruviano 2.0 — Made in — 49

MAIN ENTRANCE
A door is a panel made usually of a hard, impermeable, and hard-to-break substance, with or without windows, but sometimes consisting of a hard frame into which glass or screens have been fitted, attached to hinges by which it is attached to a frame that constitutes a space for ingress into or egress from a building, room, or vehicle, such that the panel may be moved in various ways to allow or prevent ingress or egress.

SMOKE EXHAUST
An exhaust hood, extractor hood, or range hood is a device containing a mechanical fan that hangs above the stove or cooktop in the kitchen. It removes airborne grease, combustion products, fumes, smoke, heat, and steam from the air by evacuation of the air and filtration.

HINGES
A hinge is a mechanical bearing that connects two solid objects, typically allowing only a limited angle of rotation between them. Two objects connected by an ideal hinge rotate relative to each other about a fixed axis of rotation: all other translations or rotations being prevented, and thus a hinge has one degree of freedom. Hinges may be made of flexible material or of moving components. In biology, many joints function as hinges like the elbow joint.

ELECTRICAL NETWORK
An electrical circuit is a network consisting of a closed loop, giving a return path for the current. Linear electrical networks, a special type consisting only of sources (voltage or current), linear lumped elements (resistors, capacitors, inductors), and linear distributed elements (transmission lines), have the property that signals are linearly superimposable.

CENTRAL HEATING
Heaters are appliances whose purpose is to generate heat (i.e. warmth) for the building. This can be done via central heating. Such a system contains a boiler, furnace, or heat pump to heat water, steam, or air in a central location such as a furnace room in a home, or a mechanical room in a large building. The heat can be transferred by convection, conduction, or radiation.

FOUNDATIONS
A foundation is the element of a structure which connects it to the ground, and transfers loads from the structure to the ground. Foundations are generally considered either shallow or deep. Foundation engineering is the application of soil mechanics and rock mechanics (Geotechnical engineering) in the design of foundation elements of structures.

1.0 m

0.5

0.25

0

Archaeographic House

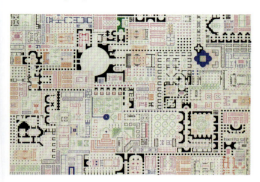

Sam Jacob Studio, *Empire of Ice Cream, No 11*, 2011-2018, ink on graph paper, 594×841 mm, courtesy Betts Project

Sam Jacob Studio

Sam Jacob is the principal of Sam Jacob Studio for architecture and design, a practice whose work ranges from urban design through architecture, design, and art to curation projects.

Sam is interested in how architecture and design makes ideas socially, formally and materially real. From nightclubs to social housing, from community centers to exhibitions, his projects are striking yet also full of familiar references, creating places and spaces with character and surprising beauty.

His work has been shown at various institutions including The Art Institute of Chicago, the MAK Vienna, the Victoria and Albert Museum, and at the Venice Biennale, where he was co-curator of the British Pavilion in 2016.

He is the head of the I oA Architectural Design Studio 3 at the University of Applied Arts in Vienna, has been a professor of architecture at the University of Illinois Chicago since 2011, and has taught at the University of Hong Kong, Yale, the Karlsruhe HfG, ABK Stuttgart, TU Vienna, and the AA. He is a columnist for *Art Review* and author of *Make It Real, Architecture as Enactment* (Strelka Press, 2012). Previously, Sam was a director of FAT Architecture.

Archaeographic House   Sam Jacob Studio   52

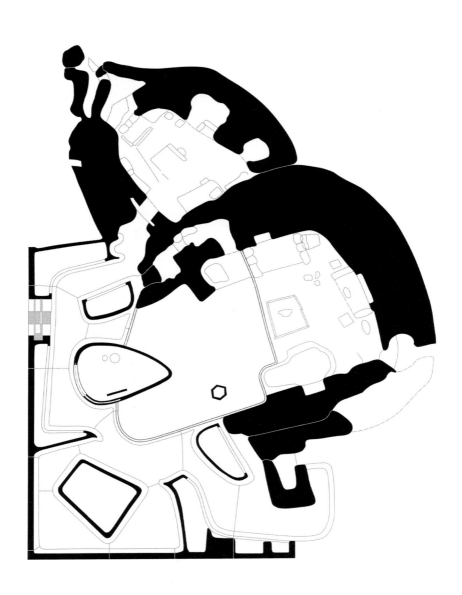

Archaeographic House — Sam Jacob Studio

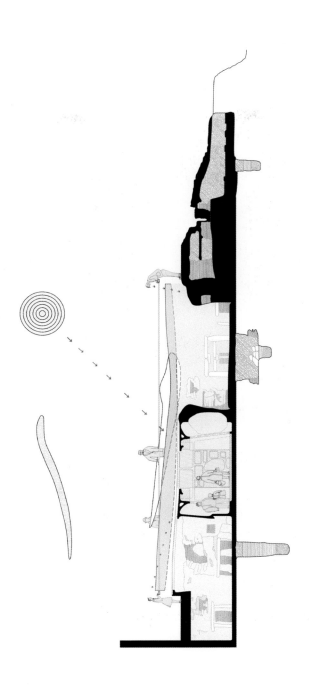

Archaeographic House　　　　Sam Jacob Studio　　　　54

Archaeographic House — Sam Jacob Studio — 55

Archaeographic House

Sam Jacob Studio

Archaeographic House　　　Sam Jacob Studio　　　57

Archaeographic House — Sam Jacob Studio — 58

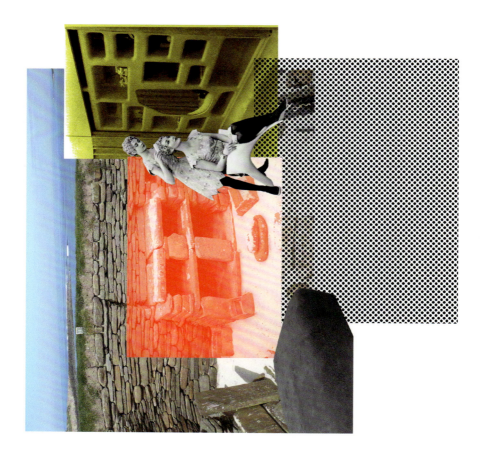

Archaeographic House — Sam Jacob Studio — 59

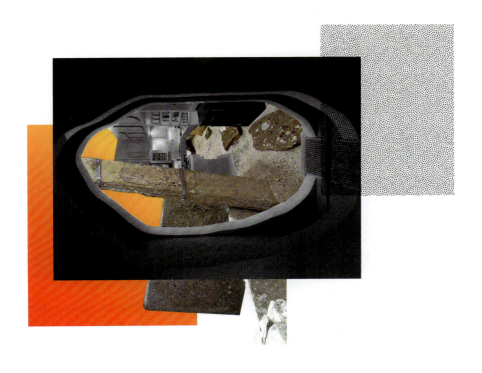

The Archaeographic House is formed through the marriage (happy or not) between two homes that bookend the history of British housing. The first is Skara Brae, a stone-built Neolithic settlement in Orkney occupied roungly 3180-2500 BC. The second is the Smithson's House of the Future, designed for the *Daily Mail Ideal Home Exhibition* at Olympia in 1956.

One is a structure that has survived for thousands of years, the other only existed in physical form for less than a month, and even then only as a kind of scenography, sketching out the possibility of future living in the year 1980.

At Skara Brae, the walls of the structures are still standing, and alleyways roofed with their original stone slabs and the interiors retain to the fittings of each house that allow us to imagine what life might have been like. Each house shares the same basic design – a large square room with a central fireplace, a bed on either side, and a shelved dresser on the wall opposite the doorway.

The House of the Future only exists through documentation – the design drawings for its production along with photographic records. Many of these photographs underscore the idea of this house as a theatrical performance of a possible future. Costumed actors lounge on the set, reading, brushing one another's hair, washing up, bathing, all with the awkward poise of catalog models. The house is constituted of amorphous blob-like spaces forming rooms arranged around an internal courtyard.

What is striking first are their obvious differences: the chronological distance from one another, one a product of an agrarian culture the other born of electronics and consumerism, and their material oppositeness – the roughness of stone walls versus smooth plastics. Yet they also seem strikingly the same: architecture becomes furniture, furniture becomes enclosure, rooms flow into one another, so that the disposition of living seems evenly distributed in both, while the floors of both seem remarkably active as domestic fields.

What they perhaps also share is an idea of fictive domesticity. One is explicitly designed as a stage set for the theatrical performance of future living, the other something we can only inhabit with a retroactive imagination as a speculation on domesticity past. Both fictions play hard with our sense of reality – that other worlds have been and will be possible.

From two opposing flanks – from the past and the future – they argue that what passes for contemporary domesticity is far from a *fait accompli*. The past and the future contain radical provocations against our own ideals for living. The Archaeographic House posits the question if its own form of futurist archaeology can help rediscover new domestic potentials.

Monadnock

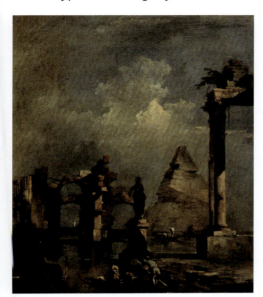

Francesco Guardi, *Capriccio with a Pyramid*, 1780

Monadnock is a Rotterdam-based architecture practice, founded in 2006 and currently run by Job Floris and Sandor Naus. Both were trained as interior and furniture designers during their studies at the St. Joost School of Art & Design in Breda (NL) and subsequently received their Master's degree at the Academy of Architecture and Urbanism in Rotterdam and Tilburg (NL).

Monadnock engages in the design, research, writing, and making in the fields of architecture, urbanism, interior design, and staging. The firm's work covers a wide spectrum, from the urban space of the city and the buildings that form street ensembles, to the scale of the interior. They focus on contemporary products, consciously embedding architecture in the cultural production of this generation and striving for an architecture that combines beauty and efficiency with the transfer of architectural knowledge.

Monadnock has garnered international acclaim for creating bespoke buildings, including distinctive housing developments and public buildings. These include a beach pavilion on the river Maas in Rotterdam (NL), a large-scale billboard installation that reads "Make No Little Plans" serving as a landmark of sorts – or a watchtower – for the municipality of Nieuw Bergen (NL), and a new visitor center for the Hoge Veluwe National Park (NL). Monadnock is currently expanding its activities across Europe.

Seven Types of Ambiguity — Monadnock — 64

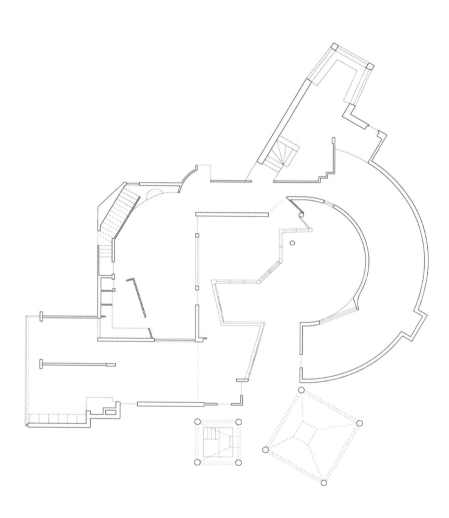

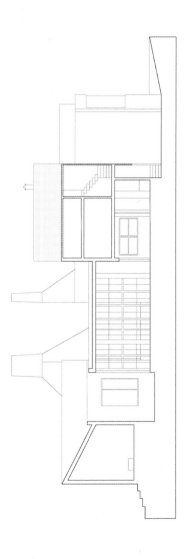

When buildings meet, they might embrace or reject each other, or start a dialogue. Such encounters might result in sheer power play, while Assimilation and Appropriation might be the decent, proper solutions instead. How is it possible to achieve a new balance while respecting the mutual intrinsic characteristics when creating a new coherence? The current encounter is one between six epic plans. Each one has been selected because it contains a specific type of ambiguity. We find them in a heated debate, meanwhile a new cohesion seems to arise.

How are you?
Hello, how are you?
How did you sleep last night?
Did you dream of me all night?

Bruther

Bruther, New Generation Research Center, Caen, photograph by Maxime Delvaux

Stéphanie Bru and Alexandre Theriot founded the office Bruther in 2007 in Paris. Bruther's projects take design back to its essentials, exploring the fields of architecture, urbanism, landscape, research, and teaching. Theirs is a design of resistance, free from any mark of mannerism, style, fashion, or excess.

Having won of many awards and contests, Bruther studio was the subject of a monograph entitled *Introduction* in 2014 along with many other international publications (2G, June 2017; El Croquis, 2022). They have also participated in various international conferences.

Alexandre Theriot and Stéphanie Bru have regularly been invited to lecture at numerous international schools (EPFL in Lausanne, UQAM in Montréal, Stuttgart, HSD in Düsseldorf, ENSAV in Paris, among others). In 2019 Theriot was appointed full professor of Architecture and Construction at ETH Zürich. In 2021 Bru was appointed full professor of Architecture at the UdK Berlin.

How are you? Bruther 70

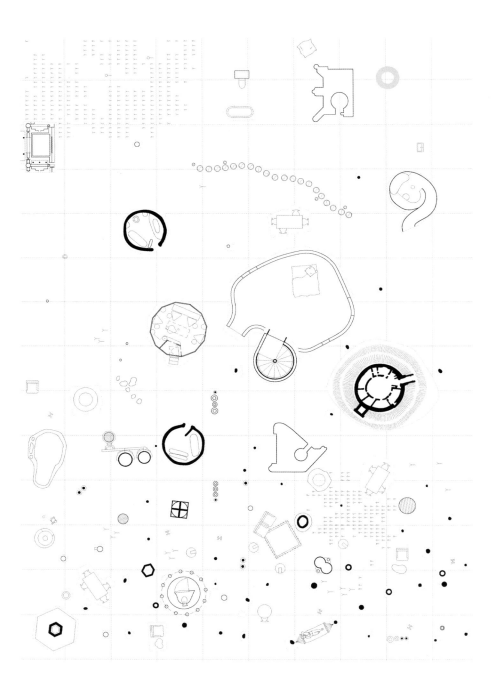

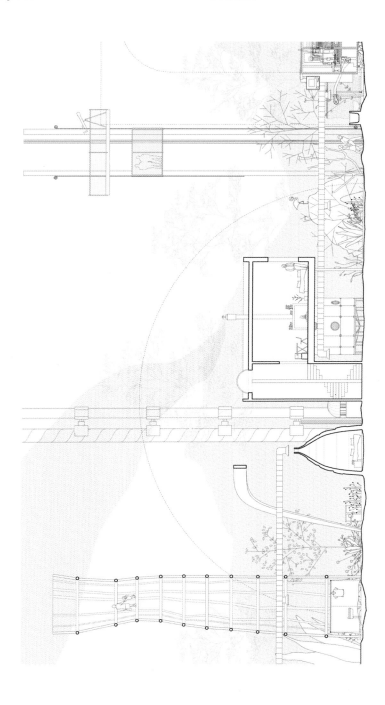

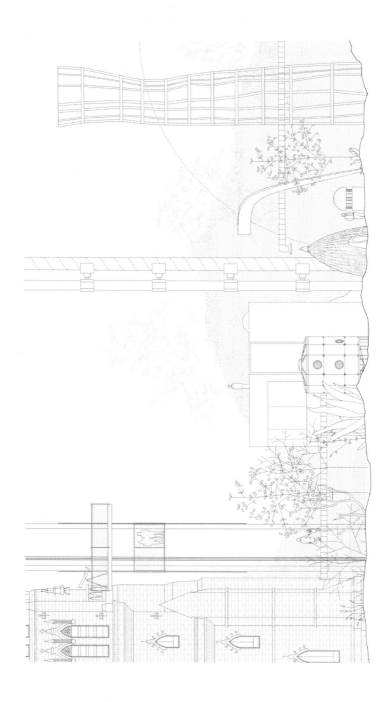

What would happen if we wanted to assemble an architectural collection identical to a collection of paintings? Would it be possible to align the references by reproducing them at their actual scale and walking around within this "spatial gallery," contemplating the works as if they were in a museum? Something is already happening. These works are not just assemblies of materials or constructive lines. They are also spaces that extend beyond their rights-of-way. Each of these works creates a form of "magnetic field" around it that affects its surroundings. In fact, to want to bring these iconic works together in proximity to each other is to produce contagion effects, or at the least the risk of a certain spatial interference. But let's take this risk! We can even bet that it will prove to be productive.

When we think about our references in the housing program, we do not think about the simple parameter of domestic organization. It is not merely a question of articulating typologies to, for example, create "building-villas" or a "collage to live in."

Let's pursue the idea of the collection to the end. And let us affirm the differences in scale between our references. Our architectural models are based on inspired design, resolving complex spatial and constructive issues, from a single line to a simple assembly. This gesture, this momentum, we perceive it just as clearly in the settings of a house-prototype as in the profile of a structural detail. We have verified it in a collage, or rather a simple superposition: the plan of San Carlo alle Quattro Fontane by Borromini (1680) is part of the profiled outline of a pillar of St. Peter's in Rome (1626). The same virtuosity in the play of curves and counter-curves is at work in a baroque church plan and the profile of a structural element. Like a fractal, the quality of the drawing is reflected at all scales. The detail and the whole are formally answered.

Our architectural appetites often push us towards "machine buildings," each piece of which is part of a general mechanics, even going so far as to give the impression that the building "breathes" and can break out of its immobility (cf. Pierre Chareau's La Maison de Verre of 1931 or John Lautner's Chemosphere of 1960). How, then, can we make this attention perceptible: to demand the same attention on objects of different sizes and utility. A collection of architectures must share this paradox. Rather than seek unification, it is necessary to make these leaps of scale visible, but also to have fun making them practicable. A Dogon fireplace, Paul Nelson's suspended house (1938) or a post by Mies van der Rohe are equally worth seeing and even practicing as such by the visitor.

This is why we have tasked ourselves with yet another challenge as to the general organization of our "exhibition." Rather than seeking a reasoned articulation, which would arrange our different references in the manner of a spatial chain (or even a rebus), we assume an almost wild juxtaposition of the elements in relation to each other. Rather than an overall plan, we propose a topological structure, based on two references that are very distant from one another a priori.

The first is a re-reading of an ancestral form of socialization. The model of the Musgum village in Cameroon inspires us without being taken literally. Is its circular shape the prefiguration of a "cluster urbanism"? Rather, we prefer to see it as a fractal structure, where the central public space is experienced as a social lung and the insides of the peripheral case-obuses as "cells" of the overall plane.

The second reference is that of utopian plans, Archizoom's "paper urbanism" plans are deliberately without scale, related to some malicious graphic games. It is precisely the playful dimension of the approach and the vagueness of its application that stimulate us. Moreover, these plans mainly draw an impulse. The strength of their lines and the sharpness of their graphics go beyond the limits of their own plans.

Our overall plan is a moving constellation, marked by several circular elements. So many points of different thicknesses, which involve the visitor's body in different ways: grazing a gallery of poles, snuggling in a Dogon box, or entering a Toyo Ito tubular sheath, and looking up to see the sky as if through a virtual telescope. In this respect, our architectural collection reflects our identity: that of a taste for the assembly of materials that, each time, reinvents the relationship of the parts to the whole. But we are going beyond the mere logic of the building which allows us to reaffirm architecture as a vehicle for a sensitive relationship between man and the world.

A House Between Properties (2018–19)

Bureau Spectacular

Bureau Spectacular is an "operation of cultural affairs" established in 2008 and is located in Los Angeles. It consists of a group of individuals who approach culture through the contemplation of art, architecture, history, politics, sociology, linguistics, mathematics, graphic design, technology, and graphic novels.

Jimenez Lai works in the world of art, culture, and education. Early in his career, Lai lived and worked in a desert shelter at Taliesin and resided in a shipping container at Atelier Van Lieshout on the piers of Rotterdam. Before founding Bureau Spectacular, Lai worked for various international offices, including MOS and OMA. He has been widely exhibited and published around the world and his *White Elephant* is part of MoMA's collection of works. His first book, the architectural graphic novel *Citizens of No Place*, was published by Princeton Architectural Press with a grant from the Graham Foundation. Lai has won various awards, including the Architectural League Prize for Young Architects, the Debut Award at the Lisbon Triennale, and the 2017 Designer of the Future Award at Art Basel/Design Miami. In 2014, Lai represented Taiwan at the 14th Venice Architectural Biennale. In 2015, he organized the *Treatise* exhibition and publication series at the Graham Foundation. Alongside MoMA, Lai's work has been collected by SFMOMA, The Art Institute of Chicago, and LACMA.

A House Between Properties (2018–19)

Bureau Spectacular

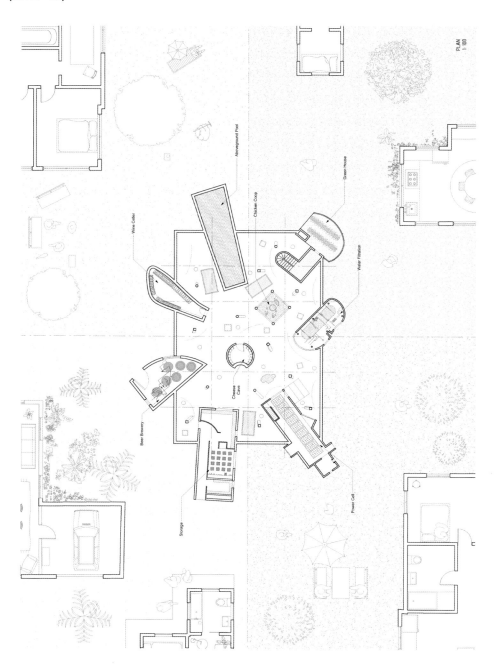

A House Between Properties (2018–19) — Bureau Spectacular

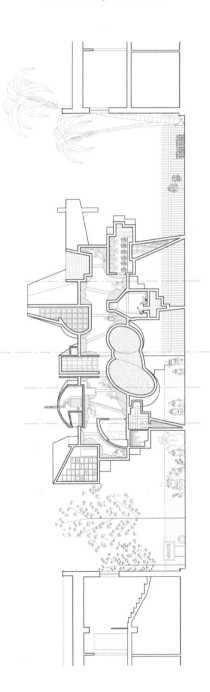

A House Between Properties (2018–19)

Bureau Spectacular

80

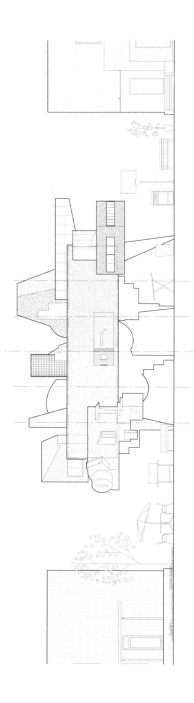

A House Between Properties (2018–19)

Bureau Spectacular

The desire to communicate identity is all over the suburban United States: why else would humans pepper their yards with decorative gnomes, Christmas ornaments, Halloween accoutrements, or other culturally specific imageries that help form a source of identity? By extension, the aesthetic qualities of architecture itself perform a similar role. The suburban United States are both a declaration of a public self as well as a security of the private self. Whereas the front of the house is an opportunity to conform through the decorations, the backyard is a location of retreat.

In the backyards of suburban Los Angeles, private properties are often physically defined by fences, hedges, or walls. Within the suburban blocks, slivers of lines are drawn to accentuate the "privatize everything" sensibility stemming from the 1980s. Unlike the Barcelona block, where the notions of private and public are blurred, the backyards of Los Angeles suburban houses are as black and white as the Nolli Plan – nothing is shared, and an ideological border cleanly defines who is or is not welcome.

In our 2018 "Yes to ADU" competition entry, we at Bureau Spectacular proposed an alternative to this urban condition. The purpose of the ADU (Accessory Dwelling Units) is to combat the shortage of housing stock by supplementing it with additional backyard homes. However, as opposed to perpetuating the notion of the absolutely private backyards for people to retreat to, we believe ADUs can help erode the rigidity of the property lines between neighbors. If we consider these ADUs to be micro-versions of "housing-plus" projects, the "plus" can be in the form of added infrastructural functions benefitting the entire block rather than the individual property only. For example, an ADU can have a dual function as solar power collector, water processing system, or collective fermentation station – infrastructures for the full block. By benefiting the full block, the backyards of the LA suburban block have a chance to transform from individual properties into collective spaces. It allows the typical LA block to dilute the strength of individual boundaries to become a permeable courtyard condition.

A House Between Properties (2018–19)

The House Between Properties (2018–19) is a version of such a backyard infrastructure – it is an ADU shared between several neighbors. This collective backyard house is a box that hovers over several legal property lines and is structurally supported by the infrastructural components that help distribute added quality of life across the suburban block. These infrastructural components attached to the box are sampled from various works of architecture – each surgically removed and programmatically transformed to have a new function parallel to the suggestions left behind by the previous works of architecture.

Although the plan of the House Between Properties permeates across property lines, its section and elevation are not so dissimilar in function from the aforementioned gnomes or decorative flamingos – it is a place where a mash-up of collective identities in a backyard may become possible; and, in doing so, the individual private backyards may become a collective courtyard.

Five Houses

Studio Muoto 85

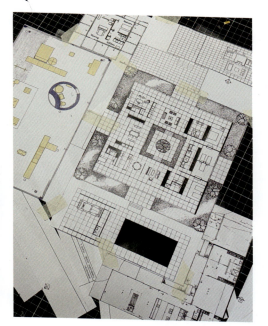

Studio Muoto, work in progress, 2019

Studio Muoto is an architectural office based in Paris, founded by Gilles Delalex and Yves Moreau in 2003. Muoto means "form" in Finnish. Their work features minimal structures that can combine different activities, evolve over time, and merge economical and aesthetic concerns, throughout all scales and typologies. They have been selected to curate the French pavilion at the 2023 Venice Biennale and have received several prizes, such as the Holcim Awards, Prix de l'Équerre d'argent, Bauwelt-Preis, and the AR Public Awards.

Gilles Delalex is a French architect. He studied in Grenoble, Montreal, Brussels, and Manchester and holds a D.A. from the University of Art and Design Helsinki. He is a professor at Paris-Malaquais School of Architecture, Head of the school's Department of Theory, History, Project, and co-director of the research lab LIAT.

Yves Moreau is a Dutch-Belgian architect. He studied at the École supérieure des arts Saint-Luc Liège in Brussels and graduated from Chalmers Tekniska Högskala, Gothenburg. Between 2000 and 2001 he collaborated with Blå Arkitektur Landskap in Sweden. Between 2001 and 2006 he worked with Christian Dior and Dominique Perrault. In 2008 he was awarded as part of the Albums des Jeunes Architectes et Paysagistes. In 2020 and 2021 he taught at the Peter Behrens School of Arts in Düsseldorf.

Five Houses — Studio Muoto

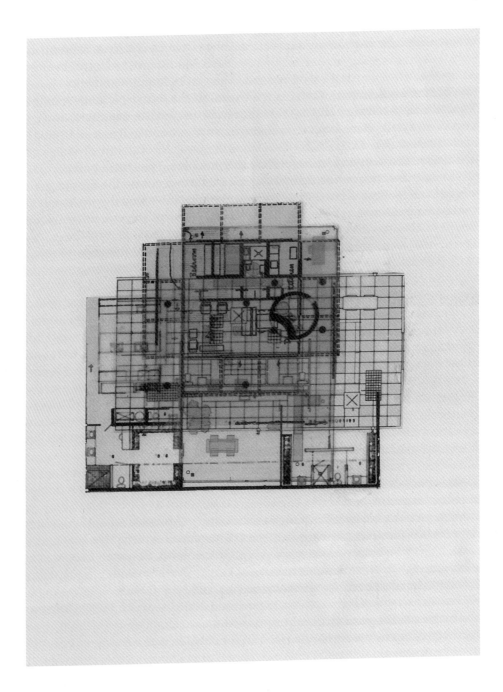

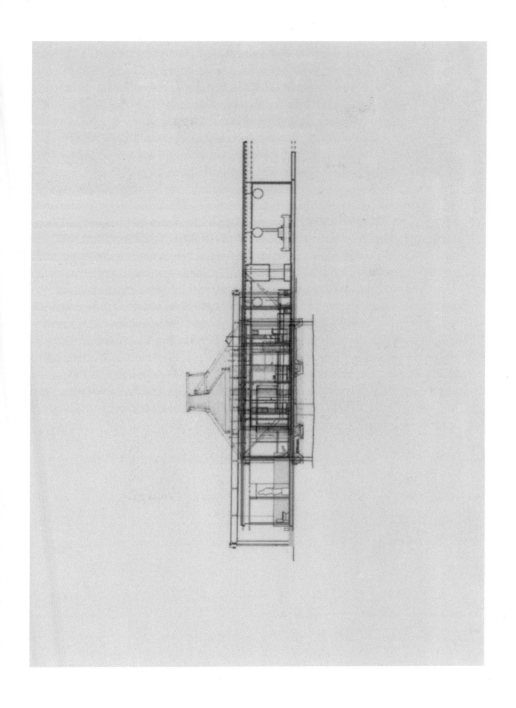

Five Houses   Studio Muoto   88

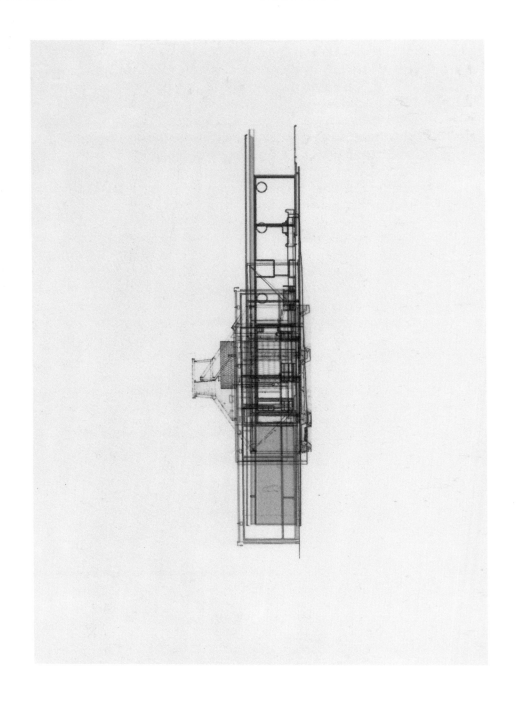

Mister C used to live in five different glass houses, which he had bought over the years for the sheer love of glass architecture. He used to travel from one house to the other. Always in the same order. Once he had visited them all, he would go back to the first one, visit all the others again. Just like Howard Hughes, the famous aviator who used to live in a series of identical apartments scattered around the world, his life was about experiencing speed. However, this speed was not like that of a bullet train. It was like a kind of inertia. A speed so absolute that it would become almost static. One day he decided that he had become too old to keep moving from one house to another. He called his architect who suggested that he should dismantle the five houses and rebuild them in a single place, since glass houses were particularly easy to dismantle and rebuild. Mister C enthusiastically accepted. His houses were then dismantled and rebuilt on a single plot. Not just next to each other, but intertwined, so as to make one house out of five. This resulted in a strange compression of space-time: a house with five bathrooms and five kitchens. A labyrinth of crisscrossing glass panels, steel structures, flat and sloping roofs, stone and wooden floors.

Mies van der Rohe, Farnsworth House, 1951
Philip Johnson, Glass House, 1949
Paul Rudolph, Walker Guest House, 1953
Pierre Koenig, Stahl House, 1959
Charles W. Moore, Moore House in Orinda, 1962

Studio Muoto
Year: 2019

Untitled Project

Giovanni Battista Piranesi, *The Roman antiquities, t. 1, Plate V Map of ancient Rome and Forma Urbis*, 1756

Conen Sigl

Maria Conen and Raoul Sigl studied architecture at EPFL Lausanne and ETH Zürich. In 2011 they founded Conen Sigl Architekt:innen. The office has won several prizes and competitions including the Swiss Art Award in Architecture. Working with existing structures is a key focus and main interest in their work. They were the architects for the Kunsthaus Glarus and are currently working on projects in and around Zürich, such as a fire station and a cooperative housing project. They have worked on different exhibition designs, such as for the Manifesta 11. Conen Sigl have been teaching together with Adam Caruso and Christ & Gantenbein at ETH Zürich and as guest professors at TU Munich, TU Dresden, and EPFL Lausanne. Since 2022 Conen is a professor for Architecture and Housing at ETH Zürich.

Untitled Project Conen Sigl 92

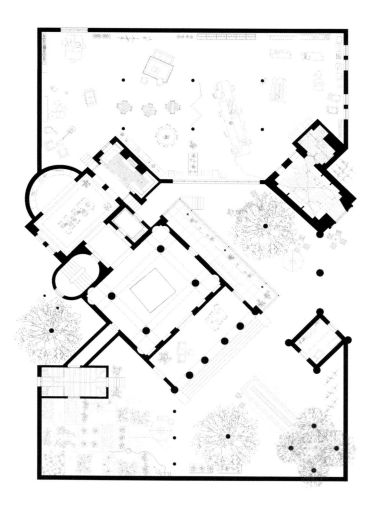

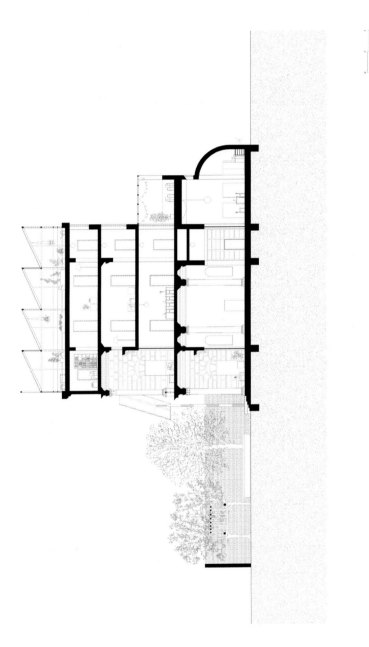

Untitled Project — Conen Sigl — 94

The task was to explore our own take on the topic of identity and to design a "dwelling" using only elements and rooms from previously existing projects from our self-defined context.

We were interested in assembling spaces that not only have an architectural quality through their form and spatial design, but also a social vision of how we live today.

The current era, also called the Anthropocene, is characterized by radical change. Technical and scientific achievments are changing the world faster than ever before.

Despite these radical changes, we think or hope that architecture can be something continuous – integrated into its long history. Well-designed spaces retain their validity over centuries. A room in a Palladian villa still touches us 400 years after its creation, although life today is very different.

This is achieved through the intelligent use of architectural elements to compose a space with beautiful proportions and materials. This is one way in which architecture can be culturally sustainable and create identity.

The size of our site corresponds to a typical plot for a freestanding eight-to-ten-apartment house in the inner city of Zurich. Most of the selected references deal in a very specific way with the basic elements of a room, like walls, floors, ceilings, and columns.

The center of our new dwelling is Palladio's sala in the Villa Cornaro with its four free-standing columns in each corner of the room. Other rooms are arranged around it like satellites.

The dining room of Schinkel's Feilner residence in Berlin is placed adjoining to the sala. It is a room intended for preparing food harvested from the garden, but it can also be used as a meeting room.

Attached to the dining room is the fireplace room from Adolf Loos' private apartment. A continuous axis connects the kitchen with the sala, the portico, and the garden.

Along this axis the large stone table from the Villa Lante is placed, which is a dining table and a fountain at the same time. The garden pavilion, which is based on the Primitive Hut of Marc-Antoine Laugier, forms the end point of this axis. This project is important to us, because the starting point of any theory of architecture is to think about the elements that create the ur-space.

The winter garden of Villa Tugendhat by Mies van der Rohe makes it possible to overwinter the plants from the garden – it also acts as a threshold space between inside and outside.

Andy Warhol's Silver Factory, directly adjacent to the residential building, is a symbol of a space that allows for multiple uses. It embodies the idea of an open workspace, a place where ideas and other things can merge and emerge from.

A fragment of Hermann Czech's Kleines Café is placed next to this large open space – an intimate, small-scaled public room.

In the garden the tent room by Karl Friedrich Schinkel is used as a demarcation for the vegetable garden. It serves as a place of retreat: the tent as an image of temporary dwelling, of mobility – but here depicted in a built, fixed, and immobile form. A space as an expression of a lifestyle.

The entire spatial conglomerate is conceived at the same time as a living and working space, with common rooms on the ground floor and private rooms on the upper floors.

Breaking up the small private housing unit into a large residential building with public spaces and small retreats creates the possibility of a new way of living together: a way that transcends beyond the traditional image of domestic cohabitation and allows for the creation of new forms of neighborhood organizations. Sharing, complementing, and helping each other, living together and yet having the possibility to live in privacy is a theme of this new housing type. And, last but not least, this might also be a way to live more sustainably and ecologically.

Our collage formulates the vision of a living form which combines the characteristics of a private villa with those of public spaces – the autonomy and determination of a villa merged with the openness or generic qualities of the Silver Factory. The chosen spaces offer the possibility of various different uses without losing their strong atmosphere and identity. That's where our interest in architecture lies: how can a space be formed, assembled, or constructed with basic elements to create a specific atmosphere in addition to its function?

Imprint

Contributors
- Maarten Delbeke
- Léon Krier
- Frederike Lausch
- Jonathan Sergison
- Made in
- Sam Jacob Studio
- Monadnock
- Bruther
- Bureau Spectacular
- Studio Muoto
- Conen Sigl

CARTHA
- Editorial Board
- Holly Baker
- Ainsley Johnston
- Amy Perkins
- Rubén Valdez
- Francisco Moura Veiga

Proofreading
- Lisa Schons

Co-Editors of the Online Issue (2016)
- Pablo Garrido Arnaiz
- Francisco Ramos Ordóñez
- Brittany Utting

Graphic Design
- Max Frischknecht

Printing and Binding
- gugler* DruckSinn, Melk, Austria

Typefaces
- Neue Haas Unica by Team '77
- Arnhem by Fred Smeijers

Paper
- Cover: Profibulk 1.1 200 gm^2
- Content: Profibulk 1.1 90gm^2

CARTHA would like to thank all authors, contributors, and supporters, especially Magizan Architecture et Urbanisme SA for their continuous support and encouragement.

Every reasonable attempt has been made by the authors, editors, and the publisher to identify owners of copyrights. Copyright holders not mentioned in the credits are asked to substantiate their claims, and recompense will be made according to standard practice.

© 2024 CARTHA and Park Books AG, Zurich
© for the texts: the authors
© for the images: the artists

All rights reserved; no part of this publication may be reproduced, stored in a retrieval system, or transmitted in any form or by any means, electronic, mechanical, photocopying, recording, or otherwise without the prior written consent of the publisher.

www.carthamagazine.com
info@carthamagazine.com